Willow Historical Monographs

The Earl de Grey

Willow Historical Monographs

The Earl de Grey

Charles Read

Willow

Willow Historical Monographs
64 Barnet Gate Lane
Arkley
BARNET
Herts EN5 2AD
020 8177 3622

First published 2007

ISBN 978-0-9555693-02
ISBN 0-9555693-03

A CIP record for this book is available from the British Library.

Printed and bound in the UK

Contents

TO THE MEMORY OF JOHN AND JANE WHITTEMORE, MY GREAT-GREAT-GRANDFATHER AND MOTHER, HEAD GARDENER AND HOUSEKEEPER, WREST PARK

Chapter 1

Introduction

Very few members of the general public have heard of Thomas Robinson, the second Earl de Grey, and even amongst historians he is not well known. Yet one first notices him, perhaps as I did, as the person who constructed Wrest Park House in Bedfordshire and his name keeps cropping up throughout the first half of the 19th century. This is not just because of the large number of estates across the country which he came to own, but for the many wide ranging spheres of life in which he was active.

You would imagine that the First President of the Royal Institute of British Architects who influenced the design of Buckingham Palace, carried out some important investigations into and preservation of Fountains Abbey, and designed and built one of the largest and original French style country houses in the country would have information about him readily available from the Institute he founded. However the Royal Institute of British Architects has no section on its website about its history or that of its founder,[1] and his portrait is tucked away unmarked in the drawings collection rooms at the Victoria and Albert Museum.

In politics, he was a famous Tory political rebel in the 1820s and his brother was, briefly, a Prime Minister of that decade. He, himself, became the Lord Lieutenant of Ireland under Peel's government during great upheavals in Irish society when "the Irish Problem" became one of a religious and sectarian nature, and yet both he and his brother are unknown.[2]

More importantly he represents the responsible landowner of the period; honest, well meaning, generous and considerate of those who lived in and around his estates. It is doubtless because of such men that the social order and political system of Britain remained stable during the 19th century, in which so many revolutions occurred around Europe and beyond. For this and for the foregoing reasons I believe that his life is worthy of recording.

Without something being known of him, much that he created has been altered and yet more may be destroyed. The first President of the Royal Institute of British Architect's Victorian colour scheme in Newby Hall has been painted over in order to be replaced by the current owners' estimation of Robert Adam's original designs.[3] Worse, his greatest monument, the house at Wrest Park, near the little village of Silsoe in Bedfordshire, may be in danger as it looses its current occupier, the Silsoe Research Institute.[4]

However, the Earl de Grey's achievements still live on today in the form of the RIBA with 30,000 members[5] (the main professional body for Architecture), the remaining ruins of Fountains Abbey, his architectural creations in Wrest Park, the Newby estate and his popularising of the French style in England. There are lessons too to be learnt from his uncompromisingly firm but open attitude which he brought to Ireland compared to the policies of Peel which latter led, in the long term, to resentment from all sides of the social, political and religious divides.

Chapter 2

Robinson, Weddell and de Grey

The Earl de Grey was not born a de Grey. Indeed, he had two names before this one. He was born as Thomas Philip Robinson the eldest son of another Thomas Philip Robinson, 2nd Baron Grantham whose family home was Newby Park in Yorkshire (now called Baldersly Park) and Mary Jemima Robinson née de Grey.[6] He first changed his name to Thomas Weddell in 1803 when he inherited Newby Hall, also in Yorkshire, from a distant relative called William Weddell.[7] Then, thirty years later, in 1833 on the death of his aunt, Amabel, Countess de Grey, 4th Baroness Lucas, he changed his name again to be Thomas Philip de Grey, 2nd Earl de Grey, 3rd Baron Grantham and 5th Baron Lucas.[8] He was born with and acquired great wealth and privilege.

Parents

His mother's family, the de Greys, were a very old family. Anchitel de Grai or Grey came from a French Norman family and was probably awarded land or wealth after the Norman Conquest of England in 1066. The first record of the de Greys' association with Wrest Park, the rebuilding of which was one of Thomas de Grey's greatest achievements, was in the thirteenth century, when an estate near the village of Silsoe in Bedfordshire was owned by a Reginald de Grey, the great-great-great-great-grandson of Anchitel de Grai.[9] The family fortunes increased so much that by the fifteenth century, Edmund de Grey was created the first Duke of Kent, but within the next hundred years the de Greys encountered hard times and were forced to sell the family seat, Wrest Park. However, on their rollercoaster of fortunes, the family soon bought the estate back and the link between the house and the de Grey family remained until the house was sold in 1917 to pay death duties.[10] Thomas Robinson's mother's father was descended from the Elizabethan land improver, Bess of Hardwicke.

Thomas Robinson's father, who had the same name, came from a family of Yorkshire landowners. They had been the owners of Studley Royal and Fountains Abbey since the seventeenth century.[11] They also had strong connections in Lincolnshire as Robinson's predecessors had been created the Baron and Baronet of Grantham, a market town in Lincolnshire.

He was born in Vienna in 1738 while his father was leading the diplomatic mission there. He went to Westminster School and Cambridge University, after which he was elected to the House of Commons as member for Christchurch where he became interested in Foreign Affairs. In 1771, he was sent to Spain as the British Ambassador to Madrid for eight years in order to keep the Spanish out of the American War of Independence.

In 1779, a disaster occurred for the British government when Spain declared war against Britain. The Ambassador was forced to return to Britain, where he met the Earl de Grey's mother, Mary de Grey.[12] They were married on the 17th August 1780, by Dr. Porteous, the Bishop of Chester and later of London, at Lord Hardwicke's house in St. James' Square.

Master Thomas

Thomas Philip Robinson was born at the official residence of the first Lord of the Board of Trade, Whitehall, London, on the 8th of December 1781. Soon after, his two brothers Frederick and Philip were born. They grew up in the middle of London in his parents house at 4, St. James' Square.

Reynolds: the three brothers, mezzotint, 1834, copy of 1788 (detail)

His aunt wrote in a letter that he was a "really fine little fellow" and heaped praise on him during his childhood.[13] He teethed well, and Lady Grantham was teaching Thomas syllables from a spelling book by the age of three.[14] From her letters it is obvious that Thomas had a happy childhood with both attention and freedom.

His father's family had owned Fountains Abbey since the seventeenth century and in his youth, he became very familiar with it. The ancient ruins fascinated him as is shown by one of his reports to the RIBA, *Excavations at Fountains Abbey (1849)*, in which he describes how "Born and bred in that county [Yorkshire] I have from my earliest youth rambled round it [Fountains Abbey] in every direction and sketched it from almost every point. I was quite alive to the beauty arising from the mixture of rock and foliage."[15] The impressive ruins of the Benedictine monastery dissolved in 1536 by King Henry VIII and his chancellor, Thomas Cromwell, inspired the mind of the young de Grey to love architecture and it is likely that without these visits to the Abbey that Wrest Park and the RIBA would have been very different.

His father became Secretary of State for Foreign Affairs when he was only 7 months old, in July 1782, and he admits that consequently he "saw little or nothing of him." He also admits that "I have only a faint recollection of him ... founded upon his picture by Romney." This was due to the fact that after the fall of the Earl of Shelburne's Ministry, and of his father's career, his father's health slowly declined until his death on the 20th of July 1786 at Putney Heath. His death made a great impression on him as one of his earliest memories was a nursery maid informing him of the news:

"I have a distinct recollection of being out in the garden with my brothers and the nursery maids when one of them brought the news of his death."[16]

After his father's death he went off to be educated in a small boarding school at Greenford, then a country village 10 miles from London. He was educated along with 12-14 other boys by Dr. Glasse, then by his son Rev. George Glasse and then by a Dr. Hooker. It has been recorded that he was treated better than some of the other pupils by both teachers and fellow pupils. He was never bullied, (unusual in the 18th century) and never "licked" in a fight. On one occasion, Dr. Hooker found him and an older boy, Osbourne, in the "Bow Room" where they should not have been. When the schoolmaster blamed it on Osbourne, he protested,

"But Grantham is here, Sir, why me?"

"Because Grantham is always employed doing something and you do nothing!"[17]

Baron, Baronet and Weddell

Master Thomas' life was not all idyllic country living and the enjoyment of wealth. His father had died when he was only four, in 1786, at which point he inherited the title Baron Grantham and its seat in the House of Lords. Obviously, a four-year-old does not attend parliament, but this meant that he knew from an early age that great things were expected from him.

1792 was a year of tragedy for Master Thomas but it was also one of great fortune. In April 1792, his mother and her butler made a surprise visit to his school to pick him up so that he could go to London to pay his respects to a deceased distant cousin called William Weddell. Weddell left his large fortune to him including Newby Hall in Yorkshire, only nine miles away from another house he owned called Newby Park. Newby Park itself was soon left vacant by the death of another cousin, Sir Norton Robinson, whom the Earl de Grey later called a "lunatic cousin."[18] He inherited the title of the sixth baronet of Grantham from him. In December 1792, he also lost his paternal uncle who left him Newby Park at which alterations were unfinished. These remained uncompleted for some time. Two years later, in 1794, his youngest brother Philip died at the age of eleven.

In 1799, he left the school in Greenford, and as any well educated member of the Aristocracy in the 18th and 19th centuries, he went to Oxbridge for his university education. He chose St. John's College, Cambridge, although his father had chosen Christ's College. However, he had the same tutor as his father, Dr. Porteous, who had also married his parents back in 1780. He graduated with an MA in 1801, at the age of nineteen, and decided to go on a grand tour of Europe.

A tour of Europe at the turn of the 19th century was very dangerous affair as Britain and France were at war with each other. Therefore, he was forced to visit Central and Eastern Europe first, sailing from Great Yarmouth to Hamburg in Germany. He travelled east via Berlin, historic Dresden, Danzig, Riga, the Russian capital of St. Petersburg and Moscow before retracing his steps back west to Berlin. He then travelled south to the other great German capital city, Vienna before touring Bavaria and Switzerland. At this point he toured the great cities of Italy, like many gentlemen did, but it was at this time that the Peace of Amiens ended the war between Britain and France. He took advantage of this to return to Britain via Paris, where he became obsessed with French Chateau architecture. In 1803, Paris was still a city recovering from the turmoil of the French Revolution, the Bastille demolished and the spilt blood on the guillotine comparatively fresh. Here, he was also introduced to the realities of life by the bad experience of being cheated out of £25 by being given a forged cheque by a Captain Cunningham who was using a false name. It was in Paris too that, later, in the 1820's after the great destruction of the Siege of Paris (1814), he would develop a knowledge of French Architecture.

Major and Colonel

He returned to Britain in 1803 and to conform with William Weddell's will (see Chapter 3) he changed his name from Robinson to Weddell on the 7th May, 1803. Unfortunately, later that year, the Peace of Amiens was broken, and Britain and France returned to being at a state of war. Britain was in imminent danger of being invaded by Napoleon's Grand Army assembling at Boulogne in the Pas de Calais, less than thirty miles away from the coast of Kent. In many times of national threat, people of all ages and classes joined the local militia, and this included Weddell. He had always wanted to be a soldier, although his family had resisted the idea. On the 6th December 1803, he became a Major in the North Yorkshire regiment of yeomanry as befitted his status as a member of the nobility.

It was also in 1803 that Weddell's brother, Frederick Robinson, graduated from Cambridge and was seeking to embark on a political career. The only problem was that he had no titles and very little wealth compared to his older brother. Therefore, Weddell gave him a captain's commission and recommended him for a job to the 3rd Earl of Hardwicke, the Lord-Lieutenant of Ireland, who was also a relative of the Robinson brothers.[19]

Frederick Robinson's political career soon took off and in 1809 he found himself opening Parliament with a speech on behalf of the Government defending military operations in Spain and Portugal. Meanwhile, Thomas Weddell was in the yeomanry, the intended purpose of which was to protect the home front while the regular army was fighting abroad. At that time there was a perceived threat of invasion from Napolean's armies. In practice, the yeomanry were also used to keep public order as there was no police force as yet.

The Napoleonic Wars ended in 1815 after the British victory at Waterloo. Weddell hero worshipped Wellington and visited Waterloo after the battle. Weddell was promoted to the position of the Colonel in the Yorkshire Hussar regiment of yeomanry on 24th March, 1831 and remained attached to the regiment for many years.

In 1816, Weddell visited Rome and from that time we have a portrait by the well known French artist Jean Auguste Dominique Ingres when he was a struggling young artist, living in Rome and earning his living by drawing portraits of wealthy visitors to the city. Weddell was thirty-four when the artist drew this detailed portrait. Ingres has caught a pose which combines the informality of youth and the self-assurance of his subject's aristocratic background. Weddell, who commissioned this portrait himself, stands against a distant view of Saint Peter's Cathedral, an important site for Grand Tourists and one that Ingres often included in portraits, but is particularly appropriate because of the subject's interest in architecture.

Jean-Auguste-Dominique Ingres: Portrait of Lord Grantham, 1816, graphite, 40.5 x 28.2cm

Weddell's ascent in social circles during this period was shown by his appointment to the position of Lord Lieutenant of Bedfordshire by the Prince Regent, later King George IV, in 1818. The position of Lord-Lieutenant of a County brought responsibility and danger, but it also brought influence through a connection with Royalty and the Royal Court. On 6th

December 1830, he faced a rioting mob of eighty workers in Flitwick demanding better wages and verbally persuaded them to go home. In 1831, a year after the ascension to the throne of King William IV, he was appointed to the position of yeomanry aide-de-camp to the new King, and in 1835 used this contact to try for a Royal Charter for his new society, the "Institute of British Architects in London." Weddell later held a similar position after Queen Victoria's ascension to the throne in 1837, and through this royal connection met one of the greatest engineering and architectural enthusiasts of the period, Prince Albert.

Weddell to de Grey

However, Weddell, after having changed his name already from Robinson to Weddell, changed it again because of further large inheritances. His maternal aunt, Countess Annabel Hume Campbell de Grey, 4th Baroness Lucas, died on the 4th May 1833, leaving Weddell a large estate. She left to her nephew Wrest Park, the family seat of the de Greys since the 13th century and he fell in love with the place. He therefore decided to change his name from Weddell to de Grey on the 24th May 1833 in honour of his mother's family.

Coats of arms

Grey

Grantham

Chapter 3

Newby Park, Newby Hall and Early Projects

The Earl de Grey is most famously associated with Wrest Park, but he was also the owner of Newby Park, near Fountains Abbey in Yorkshire and Newby Hall also in the same county. These two country homes were only nine miles away from each other, but in his memoirs he referred to them as a single estate called "Newby."[20]

Newby Park

The Robinsons' paternal ancestral seat was Newby Park bought by a Metcalfe Robinson in the 1650's. The newly restored King Charles II had made him a Baronet in 1660. On his death his estate passed to his nephew, a William Robinson who was the husband of Mary Aislable, the owner of Studley Royal and Fountains Abbey.

Newby Park is thought to be the first Palladian style villa to be built in the United Kingdom. Sir William Robinson, a Lord Mayor and MP of York, who was a direct ancestor of the Earl de Grey, asked the architect Colen Campbell design to the house in 1718. The house took three years to build and consists of three separate sections, joined by corridors. It occupies a splendid position, amidst parkland, on the banks of the River Swale and helped establish the Palladian style as dominant in the British Architecture of that period.

Newby Hall

The first record of Newby Hall is in the thirteenth century, when it was the estate of the Nubie family, who took their name from the estate.[21] In 1689, the estate was sold to Sir Edward Blackett, who was the MP for Ripon. Blackett flattened the old house and built most of the present house during the 1690's using Sir Christopher Wren, the famous architect of St. Paul's Cathedral in London. The new house was described by Celia Fiennes on her tour of the north in 1697 as "the finest house I saw in Yorkshire".

On Blackett's death, Newby Hall passed to his son and then to his son's nephew, who sold it in 1748 to the Weddell family. William Weddell was a distant cousin of the Earl de Grey, and rather like him was a very intelligent man. He was a prominent member of the Dilettanti Society and he went on the Grand Tour between 1765-6. On his return to England, he made contact with most of the leading British neo-classical architects including John Carr, James Wyatt, Sir William Chambers and the Adam brothers. Weddell's plan after he bought the house was to extend the building for his furniture collection including a collection of classical sculpture and for a set of Gobelin tapestries.

Weddell instructed the architect John Carr to add two wings to the east side of the house, rebuilding the three central bays of the east elevation and turning the facade around. Weddell also commissioned Robert Adam in 1767 to complete the galleries and to decorate some of the interior of the house. Another local architect, William Belwood, was also instructed to add the porch to the east facade which has since become the main entrance.

Weddell had no children during his lifetime and so in his will he gave Newby Hall to a distant cousin he hardly knew, Thomas Robinson, later to be the Earl de Grey. However, to continue the family name of Weddell into the future he attached the condition that Thomas Robinson would change his name to Weddell.

Weddell died in 1792, leaving the property to Robinson. As he was only 11 years of age, the executors of Weddell's will allowed him to change his name later, in 1803 after his return from his Grand Tour of Europe, to meet the condition of the will.

The "Newby" Estate

The newly named Thomas Weddell regularly spent his holidays at the Newby estates; he spent part of his honeymoon at the Newby estate with his wife.

After some consideration, he felt that perhaps that there were some limitations to his predecessor's beautiful house. He regretted the lack of a large, sunny, sitting room, and he also considered the library was far too small to house all his books. He therefore decided to turn Adam's south-facing dining room into a library and built a new dining room on the north-west corner of the house. This work was carried out between February 1808 and November 1810. Although he used an architect, a Mr Shaw, much of the design of the so-called Regency Dining Room is attributable to him, including the yellow colour scheme. He also redecorated much of the rest of the house to a new colour scheme which has only recently been reverted to the current owners' opinion of what the original Adam colour scheme would have been.

The layout of the Dining Room is unusual with arched recesses at the ends of the room. Its mouldings do not ape those of Adam but are in contrast to them. The doors to the room are strangely unresolved in the corridor out of which they open which suggests that further works were planned there.

Early projects

Other architectural projects from this date are a building in Cowes (1809) near the Castle and Skelton chapel, finished in March 1811 and built to Weddell's design. The building in Cowes was Grantham House which was sited overlooking the sea near the castle. It was a large house and was lived in for a while by George Stephenson the railway engineer. It then became the Grantham Hotel, but today the site is occupied by a block of flats called Grantham Court. Skelton Chapel "a handsome building in the early English style,"[22] was paid for by Weddell and the inhabitants jointly.

In 1816 the prison in Ripon required improvement to bring the accommodation up to standard with legislation which required different sexes and types of prisoner to be accommodated separately. Weddell was instrumental in persuading the local magistrates to rebuild the prison on a site adjacent and extend and improve the existing building which then made a fine residence for the Master of the prison. He also acted as their architect and designed the building which from 1870 became the police station, but is today the Ripon Museum.

The designs from this period are all idiosyncratic and show considerable confidence but some lack of knowledge and skill. This was remedied when he took the opportunity to study French architecture in some depth. The French capital city was being rebuilt after the Siege of Paris of 1814, "and there were many construction projects that distracted the eyes of this tourist." In a History of Wrest Park written to his daughter he describes how, "in Paris in 1822 (I believe) I was very much struck with some of the little summerhouses looking onto the little boulevards."[23] On the basis of this he designed the "the present lodges, ...and they looked so well and appropriate when finished that I felt quite confirmed as to the taste and style of architecture, if I ever built a new house."[24] These are the Brabury lodges to Wrest Park, built in 1826.

Back in the winter of 1825, at Paris, he had tried to copy some ornament in a drawing but failed. He asked a friend to try and find a young architect to help but instead he was given a list of books. He went to the Bibliotheque Royale and "was allowed to copy what I pleased."[25] He bought a folio work in three volumes of French Architecture, possibly by *Blondel, Mansart* or *Le Pautre,* all depicted in the staircase hall which he was to build at Wrest Park, and he used it as his textbook for many years. This was the moment at which he confirmed his intention for a French style home.

At this time he got the opportunity to become involved in a nationally important architectural project, that of the United Service Club in Pall Mall. Weddell was chairman of the club in

1824, 1828 and 1856–7.[26] When Carlton House was demolished by George IV, the club leased part of the site and formed a building committee to oversee the construction of a new building with Weddell serving on it. Nash was the architect, but Weddell was soon making his presence felt. Speaking in 1857, he said that the exterior design of the club-house was left entirely to Nash but, as chairman of the building committee, he "had differed with Mr. Nash as to the effect of the staircase proposed by him, and, with the greatest good temper and equanimity, Mr. Nash adopted the suggestion which he had ventured to make."[27] The design of staircases was something which fascinated Weddell and impressive examples were a feature of alterations which Weddell carried out from 1833 at 4 St James Square and in the main stairwell at Wrest Park. Plans for alterations carried out at 4 St James Square in 1833-4 by the architect W. J. Browne for Earl de Grey are in the Bedfordshire and Luton Archives Office (Lucas Collection), as is an undated "Original design for the Stair-case, St. James's Square," by de Grey himself[28].

In 1833, his aunt Annabel died and he inherited from her the Earldom of de Grey, and Wrest Park in Bedfordshire which gave him the opportunity to bring his intentions to build himself a French style home to fruition.

Grantham House, Cowes, Isle of Wight, Weddell's first design. A huge oriel window faced out toward the splendid views over the Solent.
G BRANNON, 1834 (detail)

Chapter 4

Wrest Park

Wrest Park, a house built entirely in the French style, is the greatest work of architecture left behind by the Earl de Grey. It is located by the village of Silsoe in the countryside of Bedfordshire. However, the house he built was not the first house on the estate.[29]

The estate had been in the de Grey family since the times of Reginald de Grey in the thirteenth century, during which a ramshackle medieval manor had been expanded to accommodate changing uses and fashions. By the seventeenth century though, the medieval manor was unfashionable and obsolete, and Anthony de Grey, the eleventh Earl of Kent, finally insisted on the rebuilding of the house. To make this possible he needed money, and in 1662, he married a rich heiress called Mary who was the daughter of Baron Lucas of Crudwell. When the couple received Baron Lucas' wealth on his death in 1671, they decided to embark on a renovation of the medieval house. This involved re-facing the house with neo-classical facades and of creating the basis of the formal gardens that you can see today. It is about this time that the Long Water, a long rectangular lake behind the house, was dug out. They also asked Giacomo Leoni to design a new house for the site, but the plan fell through due to the events of the time, particularly the South Sea bubble, in which many people lost money in the collapse in price of South Sea Company shares, and a new house was not built on the site until the 1830s by the Earl de Grey. The garden was also not radically altered throughout the 18th century but some small buildings and ornaments were added.[30]

Thomas Weddell inherited Wrest Park on the 4th of May 1833 on the death of his maternal aunt, Amabel Hume-Campbell, Countess de Grey of Wrest Park. He changed his name to the Earl de Grey in lieu of Weddell.[31] He immediately saw that there were structural problems with the old house. "It was quite clear to us all, many years before the place came to me, that something, upon rather a great scale must be done, if at all. The old house with its cracked walls and its long passages and its windows that annually became less capable of being closely shut down was evidently incapable of any essential repair or improvement."[32]

The "cracked walls" to the old house and the problems with the windows are undoubtedly the characteristics of subsidence, a problem that was comparatively hard to remedy in the 19th century. Therefore, he decided initially that the house should be rebuilt "upon the same spot."[33] His aunt had consulted John Shaw (1776-1832) about rebuilding the existing house in 1818 and his drawings showing a Jacobean house are in the Bedfordshire and Luton Archive office, but the new proprietor developed different tastes.

The Earl de Grey fell in love with the French eighteenth century style of architecture during his visits to Paris in 1822 and 1825 and wanted a house in this style, a novelty at the time. He decided that the new house was to be positioned where the avenues crossed each other. This was not only because he had heard his mother say that this had once been intended, but also for the practical reason that it would be possible to build the new house before knocking the old one down.

He resolved that he had seen enough of the sort of attention paid by some of the professional architects when he had been in constant touch with Mrs Nash (the architect's wife) during the building of the United Service Club and had found that all was delegated to "some clerk," and he set about drawing up the plans himself.

After he had prepared the overall designs he put them in the hands of the Mr W. J. Browne who had been Nash's clerk to make the working drawings. De Grey found him "a conceited fellow, tho' a clever one." Drawings by de Grey in the RIBA Drawings collection and the Bedfordshire and Luton Archives show the overall plan and details of some of the elevations. Later he also engaged James Clephane (Clapham) who had worked for Lord Barrington as a clerk of works. All the drawings by him in the Bedfordshire and Luton Archives are of items such as plumbing and drains.

No good building stone was available in Bedfordshire so he first experimented with a type of artificial stone by William Ranger,[34] 1800-1863, patent 1832/34 which was basically a type of concrete block used in Wellington Barracks and Barry's front of the Royal College of Surgeons. The results were not successful and they were forced to pull down, "what had not crumbled of its own accord."

In the end some French stone was used but the Earl de Grey was concerned to use local labour for economy and from a responsible attitude to the local community.

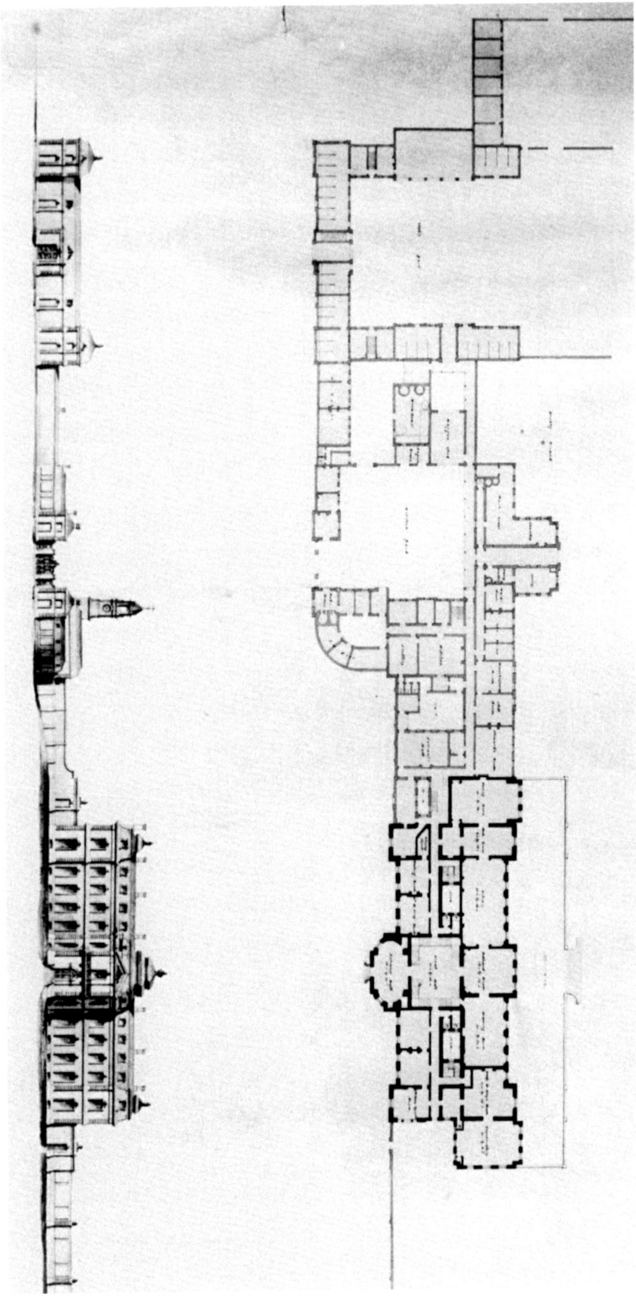

De Grey's drawing of Wrest House from the RIBA drawing collection

It can not have been easy therefore to get the craftsmanship and detail he wanted and he was "up every ladder and upon every scaffold from early morning to dusk." He treated them fairly but would not tolerate strikes, discharging those who did and refusing to take them on again. The house was completed quickly under such firm direction. The foundation stone was laid on 12th February, 1834 and the family took up residence in the autumn of 1839.

The interior was lavishly decorated in the French style. In the hallway there are groups of *putti* made of a type of *papier-maché* above an elegant staircase. The reliefs above the doors were not only designed by the Earl but partially executed by him. A large library was necessary because of all the books which the family owned. At first a drawing room was not planned because the de Grey's had always used the library for this purpose. However, one was added at the last moment as a concession to custom and John Wood was commissioned to paint the ceiling with "pretty faces." It is typical of de Grey's sense of humour that he recounts the story that, "At a ball which we gave after the room was finished, and which was attended by all the ladies of the county, amongst whom personal charms were not abundant, one old lady... was seen looking up at the top of the room muttering to herself 'More beauty on the ceiling than on the floor!' which was true."

Pevsner in the "*Buildings of England*" series in 1968 was very impressed by the house and design. He described it as a "building unique in England in its consistency of style... done in *Dixhuitième* throughout... the interiors are very lavish indeed." He compared them with the only other similar work then completed in a French style in England, which were some interiors done by Benjamin Wyatt, "but never with so much conviction." This is praise indeed, but Pevsner had been given some wrong information and the design was attributed to Clephane, thought then to be a French architect rather than the clerk of works! The praise is a genuine judgement by Pevsner himself and later attempts by others to discredit the design by citing de Grey's amateur status or by trying to find exact models from which it was copied, unfairly take away from the achievement of the composition.

In fact it is a very individual design based on late eighteenth century domestic French architecture. At this time plans a single room deep had given way to deep buildings which needed a mansard roof to span them rather than one of a single steep pitch. Externally the style had become simple with chains of rustication replacing columns of the classical orders. This is what we see at Wrest.

The main house is at the centre of the group of buildings and to one side are the stables and other ancillary accommodation, whilst on the other is an enormous walled garden, for the growing of produce for the kitchens.

The old house had been in splendid gardens which were mainly the work of the Duke of Kent who died in 1740. Since then most of the effort spent on the garden was to maintain his design. De Grey added to this legacy with the help of his gardener, George Ford. A flower garden was laid out for his wife, the walled kitchen garden was created, a French Garden was planned to match the house and buildings were added: a spectacular Orangery and the Petit Trianon built in 1836 as a playhouse for his grandchildren.

Wrest Park garden facade (above), stables tower, hallway (centre) and entrance facade (below)

Brabury Lodges in 1902. The first lodges built by Earl de Grey.

The Orangery

De Grey used Thomas Smith, a local architect, as an additional clerk of works at Wrest Park and then to build other projects nearby such as the church at Silsoe (1830-31) for which de Grey himself prepared plan, section and elevation together with a sketch for a new western tower in perpendicular style.

Chapter 5

First President of the RIBA

Architects have been around since the beginning of civilization, whether they designed the pyramids, the temples of the Acropolis or the medieval cathedrals. Yet architecture was not a formal profession in Britain until the 19th century. The majority of the famous architects such as Nash had large design offices and passed on most of the details of their work to apprentices and draughtsmen. This angered Earl de Grey.[35] It was partly his frustration that led him to pursue an interest in architecture and to design Wrest Park himself and also to become the first president of what became the Royal Institute of British Architects. The RIBA grew from small beginnings and, via de Grey, influenced some of the major London landmarks being built at the time.

The council of the Institute met for the first time on 10th December 1834 at the Thatched House Tavern, St. James' Street. The Tavern had a large meeting room and was a popular location for the meetings of learned and artistic societies. De Grey's house in London was only around the corner at St. James' Square and had recently being undergoing work. It seems therefore to have been a lucky chance combined with his enthusiasm for architecture that led to him becoming involved in the Institute.

De Grey was elected president when the "Institute for Architects in London" numbered only 13 members, some of whom gave donations to help start up the club, as can be seen from letters in the RIBA archives.

List of Major Donors in 1835

Donor	*Date*	*Donation*	*Notes*
Sir John Soane[36]	13th June 1835	£750	Gave the RIBA his portrait in July
Peter Leigh[37]	16th June 1835	£26-5s.	
Charles Barry[38]	18th June 1835	£20	Donation for library
J Thompson[39]	June 1835	25 Guineas	
James Morrison[40]	July 1835	£50	
James Morrison's Son	July 1835	£25	In same letter as J. Morrison's
George More[41]	20th July 1835	£20	

The first open meeting was held on June 15th, 1835 and Earl de Grey made a statement of objectives. By this time membership was up to 80 and a library had been formed. It was intended to offer awards to young architects for original designs and measured drawings of old buildings and it was hoped that travelling scholarships would be forthcoming. The Institute was to make contact with foreign academies and to encourage international relations with members of the profession abroad.

Twenty four years later, in 1859, Earl de Grey was still president of the "Royal Institute of British Architects," and at the last meeting before he died he remembered his election, saying, "I had no particular claim to the honour; all that I could boast was a good will to the object you had in view, and a desire to aid you in your exertions as far as my ability went."[42] The Institute's standing orders required that the president stand down each year but these were rescinded each year in de Grey's favour. At the outset there was another similar organisation called the Architectural Society. In 1842 the two societies joined together and in 1859 the total membership was 416.

De Grey made an application to the King at the outset that he should "become Patron of the Institute," but received in response a letter from Herbert Taylor saying that the King had an "apprehension that this compliance with their wish might expose him to inconvenience from the revival of other applications from other societies... which though not exactly similar ... had been produced in great number. His Majesty is advised by his Ministers ... that he should avoid too great an extension of his patronage."[43] In reporting this to the secretary, Mr Donaldson, de Grey hoped "it may be discussed for the future,"[44] and indeed the Institute became "Royal" in 1837.

In 1836 de Grey had been part of the sub-committee in the Lords,[45] which had received the report from the commissioners appointed by the King to recommend a winner to the architectural competition for the new Houses of Parliament. The endorsement of the chosen winner, no. 64, Charles Barry, may well have been influenced heavily by de Grey who visited both Barry and Dr Reid (who was to deal with the heating and ventilation)[46] in Edinburgh and it is probably no co-incidence that the Institute received its Royal patronage shortly afterwards.

The early meetings usually consisted of a paper read by one of the members and the general business such as new members and the receipt of works of art and archaeological specimens which had been donated. De Grey was careful to invite many foreign architects to be honorary members which was to give the Institute an international standing.

De Grey continued to become involved in building projects when he could. About 1840 he arranged the construction of a building for the Yorkshire Hussars, in which he was a Colonel, who required suitable accommodation for their annual mess. The result was the De Grey Rooms in York. They have a large and glamorous ballroom and were intended to be used for concerts, balls, public entertainments and meetings. The architect was G. T. Andrews, a local railway architect, but de Grey's influence can be seen in the French character of the tall round topped windows.

The De Grey Rooms, York

After his spell in Ireland, de Grey pursued the interests of the Institute with much vigour. The Builder later recorded that "at all times and in every way the president was ready to take any step that was pointed out to him as likely to promote the object and welfare of the Institute."[47] One of the ways that he did this was to promote the works of architects and of artists at *conversazione* which involved inviting the members, the wealthy, the nobility and frequently the Prince of Wales to his home at 4, St James Square where, "the tables were filled with choice portfolios, and works of art."[48] De Grey describes in his Memoirs how at a *conversazione* which he held for the Institute in 1846 "Prince Albert told me that the Queen wished I would form one of a committee to superintend various additions and improvements ... for Buckingham Palace."[49] There had been considerable problems with the Palace. King George IV had started an ambitious scheme of improvement with Nash as his architect. A budget of £250,000 had been set by Parliament and agreement to this had been obligingly arranged by de Grey's brother, Frederick Robinson (Viscount Goderich) in 1825 when he was Chancellor of the Exchequer, but by 1831 £650,000 had been spent.

A Select Committee was set up to look into the reasons for the increased costs and discovered that George IV gave instructions regardless of any money restrictions and that Nash had been making money from the supply of building materials.[50] William IV sacked Nash and appointed Edward Blore to complete the work. He completed the design in 1837 but altered it to save money. The problem in 1846 was to provide more accommodation for Queen Victoria and her family. The architect was Blore again but de Grey thought him "a very inefficient man"[51] and appears to have had considerable influence on the design himself. His sketch for the elevation and the idea of placing a new block across the open third side of the courtyard is similar to the scheme which was actually built. French stone was used to save money as had been done at Wrest Park (except here it deteriorated, and the elevation was refaced by Sir Aston Webb in 1913) and the clerk of works was James Clephane whom de Grey had employed at Wrest Park. The builder, Cubbitt, is described by de Grey as "a very superior intelligent person,"[52] and he went on to build Osbourne House for the Queen as well as other projects. The cost of the new wing was reduced to £106,000

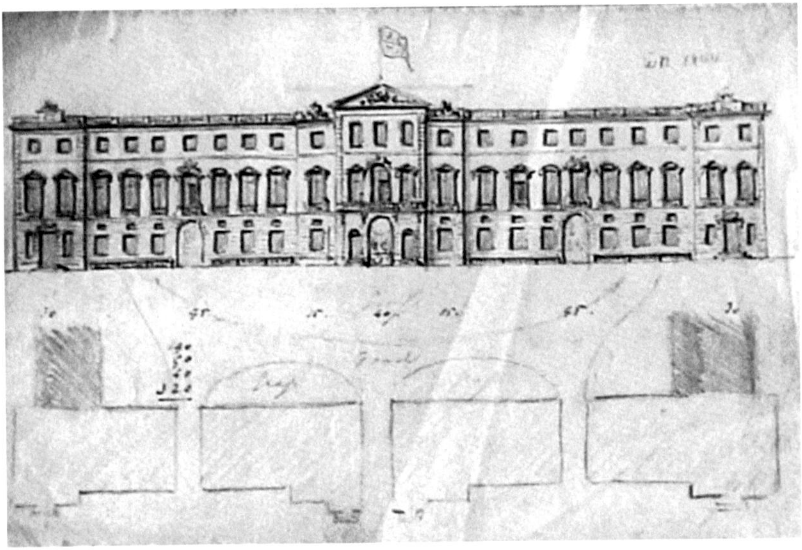

De Grey's design for Buckingham Palace © BEDFORDSHIRE & LUTON ARCHIVES

Blore's design, as built THE BUILDER, AUGUST, 1847

from the original budget of £150,000. The public thought it plain however and in the Builder it was said not to "pretend to grandeur or magnificence, scarcely to dignity."[53] Aesthetically one of the problems is a double row of windows, on the first and second floors, which are of almost the same height. Aston Webb's design disguised this by incorporating each vertical pair of windows in a single panel and by placing full height pilasters between, but it is noticeable that de Grey's design does not have this fault and also predicts the central pediment of the Aston Webb elevation.

Queen Victoria was highly delighted, however, and at the "intercession,"[54] of the Earl de Grey, founded the Royal Medal for Architecture. It was reported to the Institute's meeting in April 1846 that, "her Majesty's acquiescence was instantaneous."[55]

In return for the efforts put in on their behalf and on behalf of architecture in general, members of the Institute were expected to conduct themselves in a certain way. These expectations were recorded by Donaldson, the secretary of the Institute for many years. Their potential clients, the nobility, were well educated. "It is important, therefore, that the professional man should not limit his attention to the department of knowledge which he may profess but.... refine his literary taste, enlarge his acquaintance with history; and make himself master of topics of the day." The standard of service expected of an architect was high. "His ambition must be to be the agreeable friend of those whose interests he may be called upon to protect and whose prosperity he may be required to improve by the results of his skill and taste."[56] In contrast, the Institute did little to stand up for architects. For example, it did not intervene when Charles Barry was treated very badly over remuneration for designing the Houses of Parliament.

In 1849, de Grey gave a paper to the RIBA entitled "Excavations at Fountains Abbey." In it he describes the investigation and repair work which he had carried out. Although he appreciated the aesthetic qualities it had as a ruin, he was more concerned to investigate the various uses of the parts and preserve it for the future. The condition the ruin was in at the start of the work can be seen from contemporary engravings. The site was surrounded by thick trees and vegetation which also climbed up and grew out of the top of the remaining walls. Parts of the building were vaulted over the river and these had started to collapse.

Prints from J and HS Storer, "Delineations Graphical and Descriptive of Fountains Abbey," dating from about 1835 and showing the extent of the vegetation on the masonry.

His repairs were careful and not heavy handed. He was not tempted to speculative reconstruction and limited work to repairs essential to preserve the original fabric. The vaults over the river were repaired because if this had not been done and their collapse had blocked the river, much of the site would have been flooded and therefore lost. He also cleared the building and the surrounding area of vegetation to preserve the stone and allow views of the ruin. The main nave area was full of accumulated rubbish and debris and he employed a local historian, John Walbran, to supervise the clearing away of this to ensure items of interest were recorded and preserved. In 1852, he presented the RIBA with some coins from the excavations and in 1854 he showed some clay pots discovered buried in the base of the screen of the nave.[57] The use of these were not then known, but later were thought to be there to improve the acoustics. As the remains were unearthed, there was considerable discussion of about the use of some parts of the buildings, in particular over the lower part of the river and these were eventually concluded to be an infirmary.

The care with which the remains were treated and the respect for what was original contrasts strongly with how the Abbey had been treated by its previous owner William Aislabie who absorbed it into his garden as a romantic ruin, taking down and moving parts of it.

Much of this damage was made good as part of the work which de Grey had carried out. His actions show that he had a deep regard for the archaeology of historic buildings as well as a fascination with building new ones.

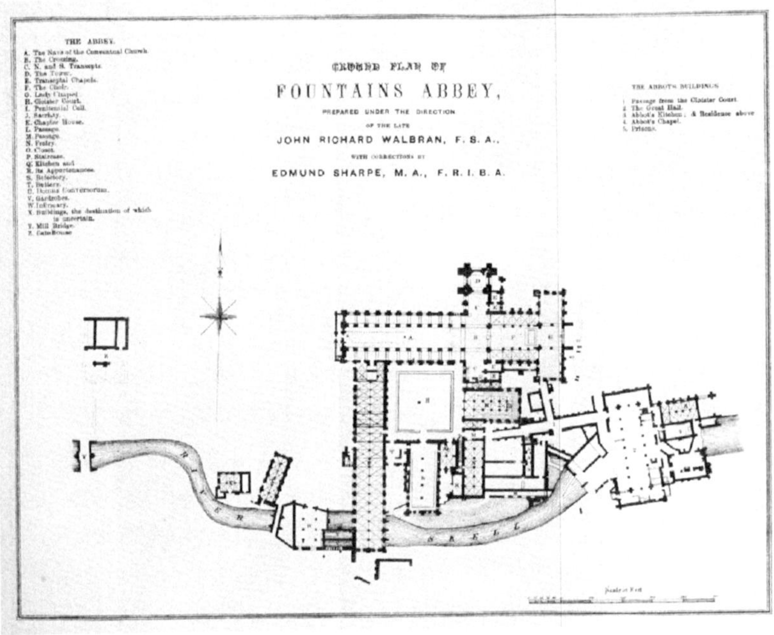

A plan of Fountains Abbey from Walbran's "Guide to Fountains Abbey." This is the revised edition of 1875 and shows the layout as then understood.

In 1857 he assisted financially in the purchase of 9, Conduit Street which was to house the Institute and other societies connected with architecture. When he died in 1859, the Builder described the RIBA as holding a, "high position... in public estimation and in that of all Europe."[58] The Earl de Grey left the RIBA as an Institute concerned primarily with the quality of architecture rather than one concerned solely with the interests of architects, and as such, it has stood the test of time.

Chapter 6

The Tory Politician

The Earl de Grey, as well as being a soldier, author, archaeologist and architect, rose to fill important political positions. His father who had entered parliament as member for Christchurch in 1761, succeeded to the peerage in 1770 and had been ambassador to Madrid between 1771 and 1779 had no serious attachment to any faction or party until, when William Petty, 2nd Earl of Shelburne, became Prime Minister, he had accepted the post of Foreign Secretary in the Whig government. In July 1782, he made peace with America. This earned him the confidence of the King who had called him an "honest man."[59] De Grey followed his father in the character traits of honesty and amiability in politics, but not in the party he supported.

The Queen Caroline Affair 1820

The Earl de Grey was a moderate Tory and clearly showed this by joining the Tory rebels in voting with the Whigs during Queen Caroline's adultery trial.[60]

Queen Caroline of Brunswick was the cousin and wife of the unpopular King George IV, who was forced to marry her by parliament in 1795, when he was Prince of Wales, in exchange for paying off his debts. George had already married Maria Fitzherbert, a Roman Catholic widow; however, the marriage was void and its offspring illegitimate in accordance with the terms of the Royal Marriages Act of 1772 as it was not a public ceremony. George hated Caroline, as he did not find her attractive, and as she smelt awful because she never used to wash herself or her clothes. After the first meeting of the couple George said to the Earl of Malmesbury, "Harris, I am not well. Pray get me a glass of brandy" and Caroline told the Earl that, "I find him very stout and by no means as handsome as his portrait," (probably due to the brandy!) The pair never did get along but the marriage was consummated and they had a daughter, Charlotte, born on the 7th January 1796.

The newlyweds quickly grew apart and by the end of spring, the couple were living separately. By 1798, she had started her own court in Montague House. She was said to be found frequently in compromising positions with naval officers, and in 1805 she was charged with adultery by a Royal Commission. Spencer Percival, Chancellor of the Exchequer, stepped in though and he reconciled the strained relationship between King George III and the Prince of Wales' wife.

However, when the Prince of Wales ascended to the throne as King George IV, he wanted to divorce her. The cabinet under the Prime Minister, Lord Liverpool, introduced a Bill of Pains and Penalties to void the royal marriage in order to stop it being dragged through the ecclesiastical courts where every sordid detail of George's mistresses would be put in the public domain.

The bill was effectively a public trial of the Queen in which the government called witnesses against Caroline. The Earl de Grey made his maiden speech in favour of Queen Caroline after joining in with the questioning of prosecution witnesses by the Lords and picking holes in some of the evidence. In particular in an instance when a witness said that the Queen had been seen at night going down a corridor towards the room of her alleged lover, de Grey pointed out that in previous evidence, which was a description of the plan of the building, a water closet was said to be located in the same direction.

The bill passed the House of Lords by a narrow margin of nine votes but was then withdrawn, as Liverpool feared it would not pass through the House of Commons with so much opposition. Queen Caroline died soon afterwards and it is not clear whether it was by natural causes.

Sir George Hayter painted a formal group portrait of those attending the trial and there are records of his sketches from life of some of the individuals. Earl de Grey's portrait (to be found on a sheet with three sketches of other people, although all catalogued as Earl de Grey) shows him asleep!

Earl de Grey in the House of Lords, Sir George Hayter chalk, circa 1820, sketch for The Trial of Queen Caroline, oils, 1820-1823 (detail)

This illustrates the comments of some observers that in spite of the scandal and surrounding sensationalism, the daily proceedings themselves quickly palled for participants and observers alike. Even the Queen, who declared that she would attend every day, sometimes got so bored that she stayed in the next room and played backgammon with Alderman Wood.

Sir George Hayter, The Trial of Queen Caroline, oils, 1820-1823 (detail) © NATIONAL PORTRAIT GALLERY, LONDON

The Great Reform Bill 1832

The second speech de Grey made in Parliament was against the Reform Bill, which was designed to dispose of Rotten Boroughs, whose electorates were controlled by dominant landowners and to give the urban middle and upper classes more representation in Parliament. This earned de Grey a reputation for being regressive.

In his Memoirs, however, he makes it clear that, he was supportive of the aims of the Reform Bill but was against "the unconstitutional way in which it was presented."[61] This referred to the way in which parliament had been dissolved and recalled so that the bill could be represented and to the "Days of May," as well as the King's threats to the peerage. Several protesters encouraged a refusal to pay taxes and a run on the banks. Some demonstrations called for the abolition of the nobility, and even of the monarchy. In these circumstances, the Duke of Wellington was unable to form a government, leaving King William IV with no choice but to recall the Earl Grey (who gave his name to the tea, not the subject of this book) to office. At length, the King consented to swamp the House of Lords with Whigs. Threatened with such a fate, opposition peers ultimately relented and they allowed the legislation to pass the House of Lords. Thereafter, de Grey spoke frequently in the House of Lords usually presenting a petition on behalf of interest groups such as farmers.

First Lord of the Admiralty 1834-5

In Sir Robert Peel's first ministry, he was appointed First Lord of the Admiralty, a position he held from 22nd December, 1834 until 25th April, 1835. He, like his predecessors as First Lord of the Admiralty, received many petitions during that period from those who had served in the Navy and were in poverty in their old age and "though I knew nor cared for them" as individuals, he saw this as a growing problem and made plans to introduce pensions rather than create a new officer class. Peel's government fell before this could be brought to fruition, but such pensions were introduced at a later date, and were one of the first state pensions in the United Kingdom.

Lord Lieutenant of Ireland 1841-44

Peel, on the formation of his new Conservative government in 1841, asked Earl de Grey to become Lord Lieutenant of Ireland. Peel wanted to be seen to provide impartial justice in Ireland and saw de Grey as the kind of person who represented this, in contrast to his own reputation.

During the Napoleonic Wars, Ireland's economy had flourished under the new bonuses of free trade with nations that were not part of Napoleon's Continental System. However, this only lasted as long as the wars continued, and with the re-imposition of trade barriers in 1815 the economy slipped into decline and scattered local famines made things worse. In response to Daniel O'Connell's Catholic Association as well as a possibility of law and order breakdown in Ireland, Catholic emancipation had been enacted in 1829, but in return, and in an act of spite from Robert Peel, then Tory Home Secretary, the Act had cut the Irish electorate to a sixth of its original size by raising franchise qualifications. However, a consequence of this was the destruction of the Tory party and its reformation as the Conservatives.

Peel was determined not to make the same mistake again and set about trying to incorporate the Catholics into the political and legal structures of Ireland. De Grey had voted for the Catholics in the Lords as early as 21st April, 1812[62] and had supported Catholic emancipation, "from the sincere and conscientious conviction of my understanding,"[63] and so from this point of view also seemed the right man for the job.

By 1840, O'Connell had moved on to the National Repeal Association declaring that repeal of the Union was the only thing the Irish people would accept. He held gatherings so big they became known as 'monster meetings'. He had always espoused resistance by legal means but was now being challenged by a new grouping, the militant Young Ireland, who had different ideas. In such a situation it was not surprising that de Grey was unwilling to take the post,[64] but in the end he agreed and commenced on 3rd September, 1841.

Earl de Grey in 1841

The problems which faced him were immense. Keeping together his own staff was difficult enough, let alone keeping together the population of Ireland. His chief secretary was Lord Eliot, a liberal minded conservative, but the solicitor-general, Sergeant Jackson, was reputed to be attached to the Orange Party. The two were in constant disagreement. De Grey worked well with the under-secretary Edward Lucas but had to protect him from Peel when he objected to appointments. De Grey's own policy was to talk to as many people as possible, show an interest in them, visit them, hold receptions and so make them feel important before actually giving them any real power. Non cooperation received social disapproval. His wife, the Countess, encouraged local traditional craftsmanship and manufacture which was intended to help provide a means out of the crippling poverty which affected most of the population. The results of this were shown in the falling number of violent incidents during the first years he was in Ireland. Speaking in 1842 to the High Sheriff and Grand Jury of Carlow, he said, "I take no merit for this improved state of things, beyond that which arises from a faithful discharge of my duty. A rigid adherence to what I believe to be right, based on a confident reliance on the support of the loyal and well-disposed, will, I trust (under Divine Providence), be attended with the blessing of harmony and goodwill amongst all classes of our fellow-countrymen."[65]

Donal A Kerr

Unfortunately, this conflicted with Peel's policy of incorporating Catholics into the political establishment as quickly as possible. In his book "Peel, Priests and Politics," D A Kerr, an historian, but also a Catholic priest himself, characterises de Grey as "reluctant to appoint Catholics"[66] and difficult to manage. This has also been incorporated into later editions of the Oxford Dictionary of National Biography. Earlier editions had relied on information given in the Times report of de Grey's death, that "he discharged the responsibilities of his vice-regal position impartially and with much credit,"[67] but this has been replaced with Kerr's presentation of de Grey as having anti-Catholic Tory views. A full reading of de Grey's letters does not support this interpretation. De Grey's desire was to be fair, but he realised the deep seated nature of the problem and that appeasement would not solve the problem. In response to a request to appoint John Howley, a Catholic, as third sergeant-at-law, de Grey wrote to Peel, "... I am as willing as any man to act towards the Roman Catholics with the utmost impartiality, but I do not feel that it is either wise or expedient to appoint an unfit man to an office merely because he is a Catholic."[68]

Peel replied with what amounted to an argument in favour of positive discrimination. In doing this, he knew he had to convince de Grey in terms of the reasons for his policy being just, but in fact his motive was expediency and convenience, to separate senior Catholics from O'Connell's movement. However, de Grey had recognized the truth about the Irish problem and Peel in turn recognized the consequences by writing "You say that no favours will conciliate the great mass of the Roman Catholics. They will not conciliate a certain class of them; but it is a fearful prospect if the whole body is so combined against the existing order of things that nothing can soften or detach any part of it. I know not how it will be possible in that case to conduct the Government of Ireland or - to maintain the connection with this country."[69] De Grey appointed John Howley, but as he had forecast, the appeasement of some well to do Catholics did not influence the great groundswell which came from the peasantry, increasingly supported by the Catholic priesthood. Many of these were trained at the seminary of St Patrick at Maynooth. This was financed by grants from the government and there was to be much arguement over increased funding.

Because de Grey talked with all classes of people he knew that a high proportion of those who went to be trained came from poor backgrounds. "An old woman at my gate earning a few shillings a week has her son a Maynooth priest,"[70] he wrote to Graham, the Home Secretary. He understood the fate of the ordinary man, "they are born in poverty and want,"[71] and how an uprising based on poverty had been extended, by the prospect of sectarian gain, to a priesthood well embedded into the peasantry. "O'Connell began the excitement of the question as a financial measure- the ardent and universal co-operation of the priests, founded upon their hopes, intentions and prospects of subverting the Established Church, has now made it a religious question."[72] The reality was that "every priest is a drill sergeant and every chapel an orderly room."[73] The connection is confirmed by a letter written by O'Connell to Rev Paul Cullen, Rector of the Irish College at Rome in which he promises that Repeal would result in the return of property to the Catholic Church and that the Protestant community would "melt into the overwhelming majority of the Irish nation,"[74]

The result was a great upsurge in Repeal support in 1843 which led to larger and more intimidating monster meetings. De Grey decided that O'Connell must be stopped and, in October, he took the decision to ban a monster meeting to be held at Clontarf Castle. He travelled to England to consult Peel who, he discovered, was on holiday and presumed, therefore, that he was authorized to act if he felt it necessary. At the very last moment de Grey proclaimed the meeting and issued 50 rounds of ammunition to each member of the armed forces. He was gambling on O'Connell's previously shown intent to avoid violence and this gamble worked. O'Connell averted an apparent possible bloodbath by sending out men on horseback along all the approach roads to turn back the people. O'Connell and others were arrested for sedition and intimidation of the people and Parliament.

In order to support the charge, affidavits should have been taken from people claiming to be intimidated, but this was not done. It is not possible that de Grey did not realise that these were needed and the lack of any action shows that he did not intend that O'Connell should be imprisoned long term. In fact, he was released after three months by the House of Lords, but he was an unwell and broken man and had little more effect on events. In this respect de Grey was successful, and O'Connell was not turned into a martyr by being imprisoned for a long time. The downside was that the nationalist propaganda machine at home and abroad made great play with the events. This, and the risk de Grey had taken, did not endear him to Peel.

De Grey also attempted to address the poverty and distress of the ordinary people which he believed was the root cause of the unrest. In October 1843, de Grey appointed a Commission of Inquiry into the tenure of land in Ireland. His intention was that it should look for solutions such as those which he implemented for his own tenants at Wrest Park (see Chapter 7). In this, he had support from the Tory landlords, who were the great promoters of improvement in agriculture and estate management. Their ideals concerning land were to see resident landlords, capable estate agents, large holdings for tenants, drainage, fencing, intensive agriculture using the latest methods with plentiful hired labour, and a protected market for corn. The farming methods of Ireland were forty to fifty years behind the mainland and were one of the reasons that the potato blight caused such damage in the country.

The Earl of Devon, an improving landlord, was made chief commissioner and John Pitt Kennedy secretary of the "Devon Commission". Kennedy, who was originally from Donegal, after retiring from the British army, had returned to Ireland to devote himself to the improvement of agriculture. In 1837, he was appointed inspector general by the National Board of Education with the aim of promoting the teaching of agriculture in its schools. He secured the appointment of inspectors with a knowledge of agriculture in each county, and established an agricultural college at Glasnevin. The Catholic, Thomas Redington, was also made a commissioner, showing that de Grey did appoint Catholics when he felt he could rely upon them. The Report of the Devon Commission in 1845 fulfilled its objectives and proposed many improvements and the removal of the sub tenant system with tenant compensation and a system of assisted emigration where necessary.

In addition, De Grey attempted to undermine the religious support being given to the Repeal movement. His solution was to have the government ask the Pope to curtail the political activities of his Irish priests. This was based on a papal injunction of 1839 which had reminded them of a sacred duty to separate themselves from all secular concerns. After much political haggling and a return of favours over Malta, it resulted in a papal re-script of October 1844, which did not have the desired effect as it was cynically sidelined and set aside by the bishops in Ireland showing that they valued their political struggle over their allegiance to the Pope.[75]

By this time, de Grey had retired (26th June 1844) on the grounds of ill health (for some time he had been troubled by "rheumatic gout"[76]) to the "deep regret of the Irish Conservative party, as well as of the more moderate men generally opposed to the policy of the present government."[77]

There is no real evidence of the details behind this. The Irish press of the time suggested that de Grey had been sacked by Peel. There was certainly a conflict between the two men about how affairs were to be conducted, but de Grey's illness was genuine and had been referred to on previous occasions. De Grey did not involve himself in politics further, and one can sense the despair of a fair and reasonable man with the political intrigue of an intractable situation. In Ireland, de Grey was replaced by a diplomat, William Heytesbury, who had no interest in the ordinary people and whose reception by both sides was lukewarm.[78] The Devon Commission reported too late to deal with the poverty which was to be made critical by the potato famine and the increase in grants to Maynooth and other attempts to win Catholic favour only had a temporary effect.

In the Oxford Dictionary of National Biography it is suggested that de Grey's views were influenced to harden against Catholics by his wife's brother, John Willoughby Cole, 2nd Earl of Enniskillen, "a leading Orangeman." This is unlikely because John Cole was known as a moderate landlord who treated his tenants fairly. Even Daniel O'Connell described him as "that rare good thing in Ireland, a resident nobleman, spending his income among his own tenantry."[79] Furthermore, he died in 1840, a whole year before de Grey took up his post.

Retirement

Back in England, de Grey was made a Knight of the Garter on the 12th of December 1844, on his retirement from politics. In his retirement, he also joined and participated in many societies including the Society of Antiquaries.

The Earl de Grey represents an essential aspect of English political tradition, that of *noblesse oblige*, in which, privilege and wealth bring responsibility and a need for commitment to the whole community. He carried out his political responsibilities with firmness, and respect for tradition but also kindness and openness towards the people he dealt with. He also thought for himself and did not follow the policies given to him by Peel, which were shown in the long term, not to be successful. His instructions as Lord Lieutenant, signed by Queen Victoria, had required him to assess the Irish situation, identify the causes of the problem and provide solutions. De Grey had attempted to do this but had found his hands tied by Peel at every turn and in this situation as he pointed out in his Memoirs, "the Lord Lieutenant becomes a mere cipher."

Chapter 7

Family Life

His Wife

In September 1803, a Thomas Weddell met a Lady Henrietta Frances Cole at a dinner party. Lady Cole was the fifth daughter of the 1st Earl of Enniskillen, who was a leading Orangeman, and had shown excessive zeal in opposing the Union and Catholic emancipation, however there is no evidence that she, or her brother the 2nd Earl of Enniskillen, espoused these views in the same violent way. Weddell was recorded as being "so much struck," with her, implying love at first sight.[80] They continued their acquaintance throughout 1804, and on Sunday 23rd of June 1805, he "proposed and was accepted" by her.

She was very popular and respected; Lady Granville noted that "The Admiration she excites is quite curious." They got married on the 20th July 1805 at Lord Carhampton's house at Cobham in Surrey and they spent their honeymoon at Putney and then at the slightly more romantic Newby estate.[81] Lady Henrietta was certainly completely different from Weddell's brother's wife whose was described as "insecure and neurotic."[82]

His Brother

Frederick Robinson eventually was elevated from the House of Commons to the House of Lords to become Viscount

Goderich and the Earl of Ripon. His political career blossomed from minor political appointments to becoming Chancellor of the Exchequer and, briefly, Prime Minister. As Chancellor, he was a great success, gaining the nickname "Prosperity Robinson." He used judicially applied tax reductions to stimulate business and always emphasised the importance of a sound economy.

He was appointed Prime Minister by King George IV on the 1st September 1827 during a turbulent political situation, which was not helped by there being a hung Parliament.[83] His wife, the Lady Sarah Robinson gave birth to a baby boy, George Samuel Robinson giving the government popularity, however, he soon lost the confidence of his senior Ministers and of the King. He resigned the premiership on the 8th of January 1828, and apparently cried on the King's shoulder before being lent his hanker-chief, which was a rare occurrence for a Georgian monarch.[84] Nevertheless, Lord Liverpool, Canning, Lord Grey and Sir Robert Peel all assigned important positions to him in their governments.

However, it was for his character that he is best remembered: willing, honest, loyal, having a careful regard for the opinions of others and an anxiety at all times to avoid conflict.[85] He always supported and worked hard for whoever gave him a political position and this is, perhaps, why he was a part of so many administrations.

It is noticeable that in difficult times, he was usually to be found staying with his brother at the Newby estate or at Wrest Park and he obviously drew reassurance and support from him during his political career.

His Children

The Weddells had five children, of which only two of them reached full maturity. Such a high rate of infant mortality was not unusual in the 19th century. In 1842 a survey reported that half of all children died before their fifth birthday. Weddell's youngest brother, Philip Robinson, had died when he was young as well.

The Weddell's first daughter was born on the 8th of June 1806 at their house in St. James' Square, just over 11 months after they got married, and was named Anne Florence. It was reported that Henrietta "...recovered well" after the birth.[86]

A year later, the Weddells were blessed with a second child, a son who could carry on the family name. Born on the 22nd August 1807, the Weddell's first son was named Thomas, after his father, and was baptised on the 20th September that year.

Mary, their second daughter was born on the 5th of February 1809, and like Mary, was blessed with good health. Happiness was not to continue though. In March 1810, doctors diagnosed the Weddell's first son, Thomas, with "water in the head."[87] In today's medical terms, this was likely to be some form of hydrocephalus, where excess brain fluid makes the head expand, crushing the brain.[88] This could have been a congenital defect or due to meningitis which would have been undiagnosed in the early 19th century. His condition quickly worsened and he died on the 31st of March 1810, plunging his family in mourning. The process of mourning was very long and arduous in the 19th century. Though the example of Queen Victoria mourning her husband Albert for the rest of her life was an extraordinary one, even at the time, people would frequently remain in mourning for relatives for years.

However, as quickly as the Weddells' happiness and heir to the family fortune was taken away, hope returned. Just twelve days after Thomas died, a second son called Frederick William, after Frederick Robinson his uncle, was born on the 11th April. He was soon baptised on the 16th May 1810 and survived his childhood unlike his unfortunate elder brother. In 1816, they had their last child, Amabel Elizabeth, however, she died on the 15th September 1827 at the age of 11.

On the other hand Frederick had a happy childhood, a successful school career, and went to Christ Church College Oxford to study. Unfortunately, towards the end of his studies for his degree, he died, on the 6th of February 1831. Being the only surviving son until his death, his parents would have been very sad as the family name and honours would not be carried on by any of his children. Six days after his death, on the 12th of February 1831, his funeral was held. Thus, the death of the Weddell's two sons ended the hope of his offspring inheriting all of his assets. The three children who died before maturity are buried with their parents in the de Grey Mausoleum in Flitton.

His Philanthropy

The Weddells (who later were the de Greys) spent a great deal of time and energy in helping the poor and the worse-off in society. The de Greys especially helped the farm labourers and poor who lived around their estate at Wrest Park. Before their arrival in May 1833, the estate and the villages of Silsoe and Flitton were in deep financial difficulties.[89] The price of corn was "too high for the poor to live by their labour" and huge increases in the poor rates hit those who could just about get by.[90] Through pressures to reduce rents to relieve poverty, Countess Amabel de Grey was forced to melt down the lead statues in the parklands of Wrest to pay for the estates' upkeep.[91]

However, by 1833, the estate had got back into profitability, but the problems of poverty in Silsoe and Flitton remained. Poaching of game from the parklands by the poor people of the surrounding area was rife. Most country landowners at the time would have employed gamekeepers with shotguns to shoot the poachers without any questions being asked. De Grey, however, sympathised with the starving poachers and would not allow his gamekeepers guns, arming them with "long sticks," something like truncheons, to eject them from his estate.[92] "He calculate[d] them to be more than a match for a half-starved poacher" and it was far more humane than using shotgun which could easily kill them by accident.[93]

De Grey also tried to solve the problem of poverty by renting out plots of land to tenants at a discounted rate of half of market value. This helped labourers earn a decent living from their own enterprise on their plots but some condemned it as the reduced rents also reduced the poor rates yielded by half, but in fact it reduced poverty by more that it cost.[94] Crime was reduced by 27%, due to these cheap plots and a gentler system of poaching control, and this showed that his innovation and care for the local people of the area surrounding Wrest Park did reduce poverty and crime greatly.[95]

The Earl and Countess de Grey also generously supported many primary schools around their estates. They supported a school of 70 boys in the village of Skelton, whose church was also designed and rebuilt by the Earl de Grey back in 1811. In Silsoe, near the entrance of Wrest Park, they supported a mixed school of 77 children and also paid the fees of scholars going to the local day school. Near their Newby estate, in Yorkshire, they supported a school for 60 girls. Their contribution would have been very important in the 1830's as there was very little money available from central government in the maintenance of local schools. The Earl de Grey also extended the church in Silsoe to accommodate an expanding population in the local area.

Their charitable generosity extended to Ireland when the Earl de Grey was appointed the Lord Lieutenant of Ireland in 1841. The Countess de Grey and Lady Jemima Elliot, the wife of the Chief Secretary of Ireland supported local products by encouraging the people to buy their "manufactures." They both frequently wore Irish tabinets and poplins, which are Irish cloths, at Court and therefore advertising them to potential buyers. This certainly helped Irish industry in the 1840's as the domestic economy was in recession due to famine.

His Books

In his long retirement after his resignation from the position of Lord-Lieutenant of Ireland he embarked on writing some books in his spare time. A year after his resignation, he wrote the biography of one of his ancestors, "*Memoirs of Sir Charles Lucas.*"[96] Lucas was the uncle of the 1st Baroness Lucas, Mary Lucas (See Chapter 4) and was a very wealthy man and extremely brave soldier who fought in the royalist armies in the early 17th century.[97] He defended Colchester and when it fell he was condemned to death by a court-martial,

He also wrote the biography of "*The Duke of Wellington apart from his Military Talents*" in 1853.[98] De Grey knew the Duke of Wellington well, as he was the Prime Minister after Goderich's resignation, and he hero worshipped him. To a modern day audience this book would seem very strange as he leaves out the highlights of Wellington's career, his military victories in the Peninsula War and at the Battle of Waterloo, and concentrates on his other achievements in the realms of politics. In the book, he argues that Wellington was a great man not only because of his military career but also because of his political achievements, his selflessness and the strength of his character.[99]

His End

As mentioned earlier, the Earl de Grey's health had been declining since the early 1840's, precipitating his resignation from his post of Lord Lieutenant of Ireland on the grounds of ill health. However, he lived on for another 15 years and this bout of ill health was probably due to stress from the fragile Irish political situation.

His wife though, did not survive to see the 1850s. After a long mortal illness, she died at 4 St. James' Square on the

2nd of July 1848 and her family were recorded as being distraught.[100] His younger brother, Frederick Robinson, did not outlive him either. On the 10th January 1859, he caught influenza at Putney Heath, and weakened quickly. He died nine days later on the 28th of January 1859, peacefully in his bed.[101]

The Earl de Grey kept his strength up and his health had been recorded as very good right up until the last few days of his life. His last entry in his memoirs was during the summer, but his kept up his public appearances right up until the last few days of his life. On the 7th of November 1859 he chaired a meeting of the Royal Institute of British Architects, and made an unusually "lengthened" speech about the history of the Institute and his connection with it. Within the week he was dead. He suddenly died shortly before 7 am on the 14th November 1859 in his London home, 4 St. James' Square, aged 78. The Times reported that the "occurrence was somewhat sudden, for up to the close of the last week ... [he] was to appearance in his customary health," showing that his demise was quick and swift.[102] One could speculate, however, that he knew his was death was imminent due to his rather retrospective speech at the last meeting of the Royal Institute of British Architects.

The honours he and his brother had acquired were quickly and suddenly showered upon his nephew, George Samuel Robinson, the Marquis of Ripon. His properties in Yorkshire also were inherited by the Second Marquis of Ripon. The ancient barony of Lucas of Crudwell, however, was inherited by his eldest daughter, at this stage the dowager Countess Cowper and with it Wrest Park.

Chapter 8

Legacy

On de Grey's death he bequeathed his property to both his daughters and his male heir, his nephew, George Robinson. Each part of this architectural legacy and the legacy of his other interests fared very differently.

Wrest Park

The Earl de Grey was the last permanent resident of Wrest Park, but the house remained in the de Grey family until the First World War.[103]

On the Earl de Grey's death in 1859, Wrest Park and its estate was passed to the Earl de Grey's eldest daughter, Anne Florence de Grey, 6th Baroness Lucas, who was the widow of Earl Cowper. She did not live permanently at the house, but she kept both the house and parkland in a good state. She still paid for a full complement of servants including the author's great-great-grandmother who was the housekeeper and her husband the head gardener. Due to the lack of a family and guests at the house the servants could roam freely around the parkland, an unusual privilege in a period in which servants were meant to be invisible.

The estate then passed, in 1880, to the Earl and Countess' eldest son, Francis Thomas de Grey, both Earl Cowper and the 7th Baron Lucas. On his death in 1905, the Wrest Park passed to his nephew, Auberon Thomas Herbert, eighth Baron Lucas, but most of his other wealth went to other distant cousins. Due to Herbert's lack of finance, the house had to be rented out to the American Ambassador to make ends meet. On the outbreak of World War One, the house was used as a military hospital for injured troops until a fire partially damaged the building in 1916. The next year, the eighth Baron Lucas was killed in action in France and the house was sold by his sister to pay death duties. It then was sold to a series of timber merchants who deforested the parkland and returned the outermost lying parts of the estate to agricultural use.

However, after World War Two, the house and remaining parkland was saved by the Ministry of Works by its purchase for the nation. The estate became home of the National Institute of Agricultural Engineering, later to become the Silsoe Research Institute. However, they have very recently vacated the estate and today the buildings stand empty. The gardens are still maintained by English Heritage and are open to the public.

Through Wrest Park, de Grey influenced future design by popularising French Architectural styles, which had become unpopular after the Napoleonic Wars. The French style of building, called "Second Empire," came to be one of the many styles used after 1850 to design buildings. With its mansard roofs and neoclassical tiered storeys it was very useful for large urban buildings such as the Langham Hotel in London or the Grand Hotel in Scarborough.

The title Earl de Grey was passed on to George Samuel Robinson, the first son of de Grey's brother Viscount

Goderich. George Robinson was a famous liberal politician, and in 1859 he was elevated to the House of Lords when he inherited the titles of Goderich and de Grey. He remained active in politics, serving as a minister in many ministries' including in several of Gladstone's. In 1911, on the death of George Robinson, he passed his titles onto his son Frederick Robinson, who had no male heirs. Thus, in 1923, the title of the Earl de Grey, Viscount Goderich, Baron Grantham and Baronet Grantham all became extinct.

Newby Park

Newby Park plus the 100 acres around it was sold by the Earl de Grey to George Hudson, an infamous investor in railways, in 1845. "The Railway King," as he was known, was a self-made man and was suspected of improper dealings during the railway share crash of 1847, and it is no surprise that he did not continue the Earl de Grey's philanthropic work around the estate.

Newby Park was renamed Baldersby Park and in 1900 it was sold to John Brennand, a cotton magnate and the house remained a private country house until 1927, at which point, like many other country houses, it was converted for an institutional use. Newby Park was turned into a private boarding school for girls called Queen Mary's School after the wife of King George V. During the Second World War, the house was requisitioned by the government and the Canadian Air Force was moved to Baldersby Park. Canadian armed personnel are still blamed for damaging the building's clock tower; during hostilities they frequently used to use the clock and weathervane for target practice!

After the war the house was returned to school use and has continued to this present day. In a program of renovation the damaged clock has just been mended and Brennand's banners are once again hanging in the Baldersby Park chapel having been returned to the school by a former pupil of the school who discovered them in an auction in South Africa.

Newby Hall

As described in Chapter 7, Newby Hall was given by the Earl de Grey to his second daughter, Mary de Grey when she married her husband, Henry Vyner of Gautby (in Lincolnshire.) His nephew, the second Marquis of Ripon, used to stay regularly in the house, and loved its game park. Between 1859 and his death he killed a total of 556,813 animals in the park, and died "in a field of heather" after killing 65 pheasants and a swift.[104] She seems to have had little respect for elegance and classical architecture, rather like her father who preferred the style of 18th century French châteaux.

The greatest change to Newby Hall by Mary de Grey was the commissioning of the architect William Burges (1827-1881) to build a church in the parklands to commemorate the death of her son, Frederick Vyner, who was brutally murdered by Greek brigands. Mary also commissioned Burges to build new piers for the main entrance gates to the Park. Her son then added the Victorian Wing and a new Billiards Room in order to improve the proportions of the house from the outside. The house was not required for the war effort and has remained until today a private residence. The garden has been remodelled as in the view of the present owner's grandfather it was "an exceptionally beautiful home but no garden to speak of" like a "lovely picture but no frame." Today Richard Compton, a direct descendent of the Earl de Grey, owns the house and the house is open to the public, though due to some "restoration" the Earl de Grey's Victorian colour scheme has been over painted in favour of Robert Adam's original, in my view to its detriment, though de Grey's colour scheme has been retained in his dining room.[105]

The RIBA

The Earl de Grey agreed to become the President of the "Institute of British Architects in London" because of his concern to see an improvement in the quality of architectural service provided to clients. He had not been happy with Nash's service when involved in the building of the United Service Club and because of this he often took the architectural lead himself in projects such as Wrest Park. In line with this concern, the Institute remained a truly professional association concerned principally with the quality of architecture instead of being solely a "professional Trade Union" such as the British Medical Association is occasionally accused of being. Far from aggressively protecting architect's rights like the British health professionals' association does for medical staff, the RIBA promotes architects, architecture in general and the conservation of historic buildings. The Royal Gold Medal for Architecture, founded by de Grey, is still given out annually, and has been awarded to many famous architects both British and foreign.[106] It is now Britain's main architectural professional organisation with over 30,000 members.[107]

His Political Legacy

De Grey's leadership of the Admiralty in the 1830's, albeit brief, also lead to change for the better. In 1853, partially due to de Grey's idea, naval pensions were introduced on a formal basis. This has improved the welfare of many ex-servicemen who fought for the British Empire from the 19th century up to the present day.

However, the situation in Ireland, after de Grey resigned as its Lord-Lieutenant, did not improve. After his resignation, the violence and controversy that de Grey had reduced returned with a vengeance. Daniel O'Connell had been forced into obscurity, however, a new organisation, Young Ireland, continued its opposition to British Rule. The leaders of Young Ireland were both Protestant and Catholic showing the opposition to Peel's policy from both sides of the religious divide. Civil unrest returned, further provoked by the Irish Potato famine, which had started in 1845, killing hundreds of thousands and forcing many more to emigrate.

The Irish Nationalist Party was then formed and with the help of the Liberal Prime Minister William Gladstone, tried to get the Home Rule Bill passed. However, this was defeated and led to the Liberal Unionists breaking from the Liberal party in 1886 and dashing the hope of independence for another generation.

When the Liberals returned to power in 1906 with a huge majority, they tried again to pass Home Rule for Ireland, however, these plans were delayed on the outbreak of the First World War. The War Effort did not unite Ireland and unrest continued culminating in the failed Easter Rising of 1916, in which Irish revolutionaries aided by the German military authorities tried to seize the centre of Dublin. After the Armistice, in November 1918, Ireland was plunged into Civil War, the Irish Republican Army (the IRA) fighting against the infamous, albeit unfairly represented, "Black and Tans." Irish independence was given in 1921 after the British had virtually lost control of rural Ireland.

The bloodshed and violence surrounding the independence of Ireland could have arguably been avoided if de Grey's policy of firmness but open communication had been followed in preference to Peel's policy of appeasement. Peel tried to appoint Catholics without looking at their other attributes and this alienated both the Catholic and Protestant populations in Ireland. It eventually encouraged demands for Home Rule which led to violent conflict and this has continued until recently in Northern Ireland. Now, however, the cutting off of funds from America because of other terrorist events together with the political will for change has implemented, accidentally, de Grey's firm but communicative policy and has resulted in the IRA's disarmament and hopefully the sharing of power by both the Unionists and Republicans in Northern Ireland.

In conclusion, the Earl de Grey left a legacy in many areas, from politics to Architecture, and therefore it is not surprising that his name appears so many times in historical records despite him being virtually unknown as an historical figure.

Earl de Grey

Earl de Grey: official portrait, signed momento and the photograph (top left) from which they were taken

Chapter 9

Conclusion

The Earl de Grey in his memoirs described his life as having "...no striking events connected with it" and that it "had little to boast of in public or private."[108] As I have shown in this book, this is far from the reality.

De Grey achieved many great and important things in his life. He founded an important Royal Institute, which survives today with great strength. Through the institute and his designs on his estates such as Wrest Park he influenced architecture and architectural design beyond his death. De Grey and his wife also helped countless ordinary people around their estates and in Ireland and was certainly a popular person among the general public of the time. He did his duty to Britain in the Admiralty and he promoted peace in Ireland even although his policy was at variance with that of Peel throughout his appointment.

De Grey, although not a key figure in the Tory party, was part of the movement towards modern "One Nation" conservatism. When de Grey was born in 1781, the Tory Party was a political elite that mainly consisted of the aristocracy and the land owning classes. Their political "ideology" was simply to maintain the status quo, which was to keep the aristocracy in economic and political power over the poor who were kept in poverty. The process of reforming the Tories started with a Whig, Sir Edmund Burke the philosopher, writing the "*Reflections on the Revolution in France*" which founded the basis of modern conservatism. Burke wrote that revolutions such as the French Revolution were bad for society and the welfare of the people and instead there should be social change, but gradual change firmly based on traditional institutions such as the monarchy or parliament.[109] It is very likely that de Grey read this book as in the 1790's he was a student and the French Revolution was a hotly debated subject at that time. There is also evidence that de Grey believed in this new breed of conservatism rather than Toryism. He opposed the Bill of Pains and Penalties, showing that he believed in family values rather than supporting King George IV's divorce. He was a supporter of electoral reform in the Reform Bill of 1832, yet he opposed the way in which it was presented, for the King threatening to flood the House of Lords with pro-Reform Bill peers was a constitutional shift towards the superiority of the House of Commons rather than equity of the Houses. Therefore, this shows that he believed in slow gradual change with respect for the status of old institutions.

He showed other characteristics of the "One Nation" Conservatives, a movement that was not named as such until at least a decade after his death. He believed in an organic society in which everyone is interdependent and in social unity rather than social conflict between the rich and the poor.[110] He financed many institutions that helped poor people around his estates and in Ireland and showed compassion instead of indifference, unlike many other aristocrats, for his estate workers. His fair allotment allocations and the following fall in crime also show his belief that the rich and poor can live in harmony together in one society or "One Nation."

His character, that of openness, honesty, directness and standing up for that in which one believes, is one for which he deserves to be remembered. When one searches for the essential English or British character, this is a key part of it. It is perhaps something missing in modern political life; if all politicians were de Greys, Britain would be a far more stable, reassuring and fairer place in which to live.

Earl de Grey's monument in the de Grey Mausoleum, Flitton Church

The de Grey Family Tree

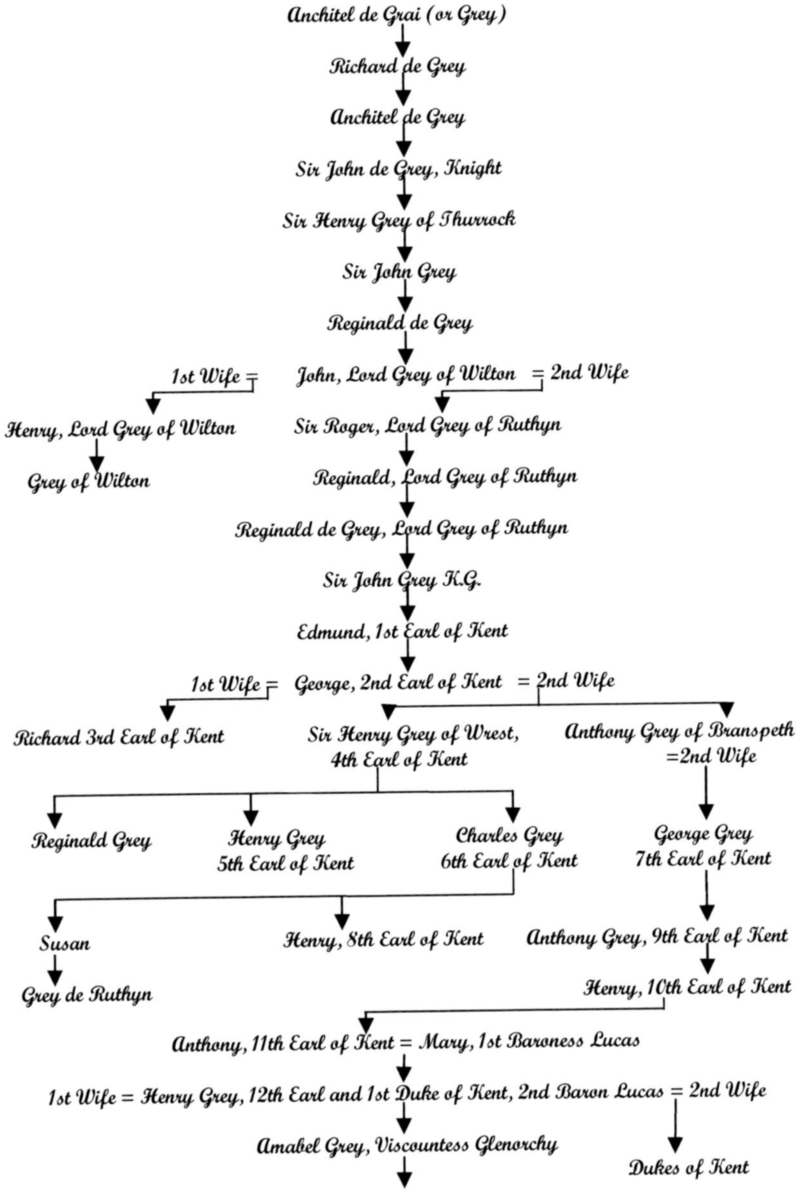

Jemima, Marchioness Grey Countess of Hardwicke, = Philip Yorke,
3rd Baroness Lucas Second Earl of Hardwicke

Amabel, Countess de Grey,
4th Baroness Lucas

Mary Jemima, = Thomas Philip Robinson
Lady Grantham 1st Earl de Grey

Frederick Robinson Marquis Of Ripon

THOMAS PHILIP ROBINSON (then WEDDELL then DE GREY)
Lord Grantham, 2nd Earl de Grey, 5th Baron Lucas

G.S. Robinson M. of Ripon

Frederick Robinson M. of Ripon

Earl Cowper = Anne Florence, 6th Baroness Lucas

Mary = Henry Vyner

Francis Thomas de Grey,
Earl Cowper, 7th Baron Lucas

Auberon Herbert = Florence Amabel

Other Issue

Auberon Thomas Herbert,
8th Baron Lucas

H.J. Cooper = Nanino, 9th Baroness Lucas

Index

Endnotes

Chapter 1

[1] www.architecture.com
[2] *Oxford Dictionary of National Biography* (2004)
[3] *Newby Hall*, Richard Compton (2004)
[4] *Wrest Park*, Nicola Smith (1995)
[5] RIBA website, www.riba.org.uk

Chapter 2

[6] *Wrest Park*, Nicola Smith (1995)
[7] *Oxford Dictionary of National Biography* (2004)
[8] *Oxford Dictionary of National Biography* (2004)
[9] De Grey family tree based on author's research at the Luton and Bedfordshire Archives
[10] *Wrest Park*, Nicola Smith (1995)
[11] *Department of the Environment Official Handbook: Fountains Abbey*, R. Gilyard-Beer (1970)
[12] *Transcript of the Memoirs of the Earl de Grey,* the Earl de Grey (1859) (not published)
[13] Letter to Lady Grantham from Marchioness de Grey, 15 Sept. 1782
[14] Letter to Lady Grantham from A. Polwarth 15 Sept. 1782
[15] *Excavations at Fountains Abbey,* the Earl de Grey (1849)
[16] *Transcript of the Memoirs of the Earl de Grey,* the Earl de Grey (1859) (not published)
[17] *Transcript of the Memoirs of the Earl de Grey,* the Earl de Grey (1859) (not published)
[18] *Transcript of the Memoirs of the Earl de Grey,* the Earl de Grey (1859) (not published)
[19] *Prosperity Robinson: The Life of Viscount Goderich*, W. D. Jones 1967

Chapter 3

[20] *Transcript of the Memoirs of the Earl de Grey,* the Earl de Grey (1859) (not published)
[21] *Newby Hall*, Richard Compton (2004)
[22] *A Topographical Dictionary of England* (1848)
[23] *Earl de Grey's History of Wrest Park to his daughter Anne* (1846) (not published)

[24] *Earl de Grey's History of Wrest Park to his daughter Anne* (1846) (not published)
[25] *Earl de Grey's History of Wrest Park to his daughter Anne* (1846) (not published)
[26] *History of the United Service Club*, Major-General Sir Louis C. Jackson, (1937) p. 125.
[27] *The Builder* 23 May 1857
[28] Bedfordshire and Luton Archives L33/272 NEG 1012

Chapter 4

[29] *Wrest Park*, Nicola Smith (1995)
[30] *Wrest Park*, Nicola Smith (1995)
[31] *Oxford Dictionary of National Biography* (2004)
[32] *Earl de Grey's History of Wrest Park to his daughter Anne* (1846) (not published)
[33] *Earl de Grey's History of Wrest Park to his daughter Anne* (1846) (not published). Other unaccredited quotes in this chapter are also from this source.
[34] *Modern English Biographies*, F Boase,

Chapter 5

[35] *Earl de Grey's History of Wrest Park to his daughter Anne* (1846) (not published)
[36] Letter to President of RIBA from Sir John Soames, dated 13th June 1835
[37] Letter to Council of RIBA from Peter Leigh, dated 16th June 1835
[38] Letter to Council of RIBA from Charles Barry, dated 18th June 1835
[39] Letter to Council of RIBA from J Thompson, dated June 1835
[40] Letter to Council of RIBA from James Morrison, dated July 1835
[41] Letter to Council of RIBA from George More, dated 20th July 1835
[42] Times 9 Nov 1859, p.7.
[43] Letter Taylor to de Grey 20 May, 1835
[44] Letter de Grey to Donaldson 21 May, 1835
[45] The Times 3 Mar, 1836
[46] Letter Barry to Donaldson April 1836.
[47] *The Builder,* 19 Nov, 1859
[48] *The Builder,* 3 May 1845
[49] *Transcript of the Memoirs of the Earl de Grey,* the Earl de Grey (1859) (not published)

[50] *Minutes of Evidence, Select Committe on Windsor Castle and Buckingham Palace*, 5 Mar 1831
[51] *Transcript of the Memoirs of the Earl de Grey,* the Earl de Grey (1859) (not published)
[52] *Transcript of the Memoirs of the Earl de Grey,* the Earl de Grey (1859) (not published)
[53] *The Builder,* 8 Aug 1847
[54] *The Builder,* 19 Nov, 1859
[55] *The Builder,* 25 Apr, 1846
[56] *Architectural Maxims & Theorems,* Professor Donaldson (1847)
[57] Notes and Queries 11 Nov, 1854, p.386.
[58] *The Builder,* 19 Nov, 1859
[59] Letter King to Shelburne, 12 Jul 1782.

Chapter 6

[60] *Oxford Dictionary of National Biography* (2004)
[61] *Transcript of the Memoirs of the Earl de Grey,* the Earl de Grey (1859) (not published)
[62] Hansard (1st ser.) xxiv 360
[63] Letter de Grey to Elizabeth Sophia Lawrence, Ripon Papers, 16 Jun 1813(?) BM 40862.
[64] Letter de Grey to Peel 18 May 1841, Add MSS 40477, f.3.
[65] The Times, 25 Mar 1842, p.5.
[66] *Peel, Priests and Politics*, DA Kerr, (1982), p.389.
[67] The Times, 15 Nov 1859, p.7.
[68] Letter de Grey to Peel 18 Aug 1843, Add MSS 40478, ff119-20.
[69] Letter Peel to de Grey 22 Aug 1843, Add MSS 40478, ff160-6.
[70] Letter de Grey to Graham, 27 Feb 1844.
[71] Letter de Grey to Graham, 27 Feb 1844.
[72] Letter de Grey to Peel 17 Jun 1843.
[73] Letter de Grey to Graham 12 Jun 1843.
[74] Letter O'Connell to Rev Cullen 9 May 1842.
[75] *States of Mind*, O MacDonagh, (1983), p.96.
[76] The Times, 20 Jun, 1842, p.7.
[77] The Times, 22 June 1844, p.6.
[78] The Times, 31 Jan 1845, p.6.
[79] Enniskillean Papers, Public Record Office, N Ireland.

Chapter 7

[80] *Transcript of the Memoirs of the Earl de Grey,* the Earl de Grey (1859) (not published)
[81] Ibid.
[82] www.number-10.gov.uk
[83] *Prosperity Robinson,* W D Jones (1967), p.167.
[84] *Prosperity Robinson,* W D Jones (1967), p.203.
[85] *Prosperity Robinson,* W D Jones (1967), p.279.
[86] *Transcript of the Memoirs of the Earl de Grey,* the Earl de Grey (1859) (not published)
[87] Ibid.
[88] *The British Medical Association Complete Family Health Encyclopaedia* (1992)
[89] Bedfordshire and Luton Archives, L39/11/215/75
[90] Bedfordshire and Luton Archives, L30/11/215/119
[91] Bedfordshire and Luton Archives, L30/11/132/6
[92] The Times, 20th November 1832, p.6.
[93] Ibid.
[94] Report of 1837-38 Select Committee on the Poor Law
[95] Minutes of 1837-38 Select Committee on the Poor Law
[96] *Memoirs of Sir Charles Lucas*, the Earl de Grey (1845)
[97] Ibid.
[98] *The Duke of Wellington apart from his Military Talents*, the Earl de Grey (1853)
[99] Ibid.
[100] Author's research at the De Grey Mausoleum in Flitton.
[101] *Prosperity Robinson,* W D Jones (1967), p. 274
[102] The Times, 15 Nov, 1859

Chapter 8

[103] *Wrest Park*, Nicola Smith (1995)
[104] Author's Research at Newby Hall
[105] *Newby Hall*, Richard Compton (2004)
[106] www.architecture.com
[107] RIBA website, www.riba.org.uk

Chapter 9

[108] *Transcript of the Memoirs of the Earl de Grey,* the Earl de Grey (1859) (not published)
[109] *Reflections on the Revolution in France*, Edmund Burke (1790)
[110] Ibid.